BILLY JOEL
EASY PIANO COLLECTION

ISBN: 978-0-7935-3755-6

Visit Hal Leonard Online at
www.halleonard.com

Contact us:
Hal Leonard
7777 West Bluemound Road
Milwaukee, WI 53213
Email: info@halleonard.com

In Europe, contact:
Hal Leonard Europe Limited
42 Wigmore Street
Marylebone, London, W1U 2RN
Email: info@halleonardeurope.com

In Australia, contact:
Hal Leonard Australia Pty. Ltd.
4 Lentara Court
Cheltenham, Victoria, 3192 Australia
Email: info@halleonard.com.au

JUST THE WAY YOU ARE

Words and Music by
BILLY JOEL

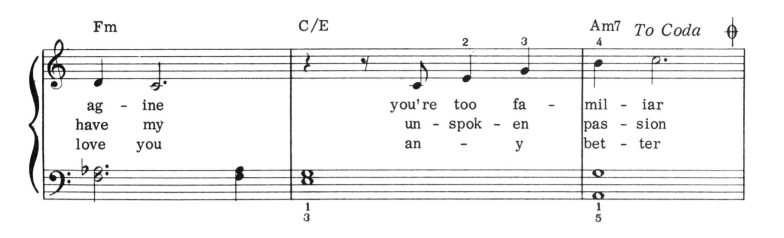

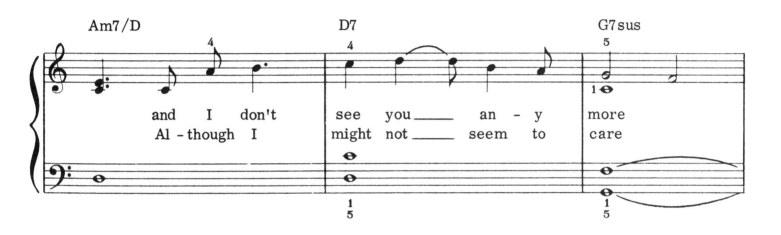

5

LEAVE A TENDER MOMENT ALONE

Words and Music by
BILLY JOEL

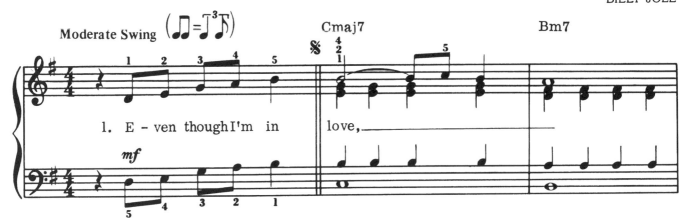

1. E-ven though I'm in love, _____

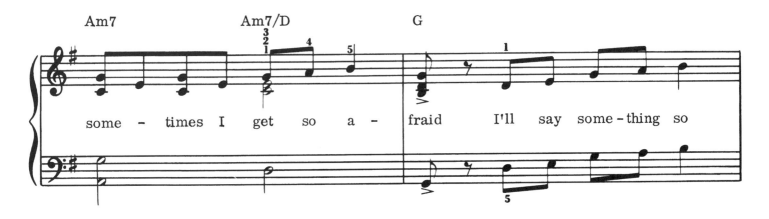

some - times I get so a - fraid I'll say some-thing so

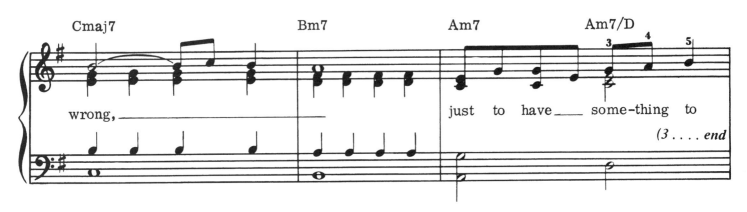

wrong, _____ just to have _____ some-thing to

(3 . . . . end

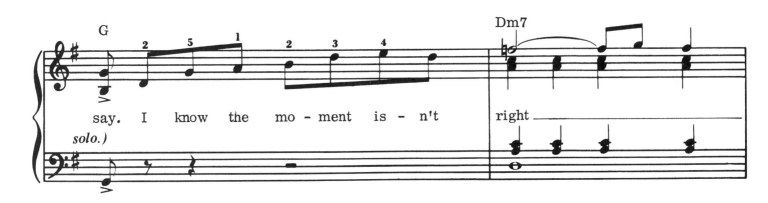

say. I know the mo - ment is - n't right _____

solo.)

known. It's un - de - ni - a - bly real; _____

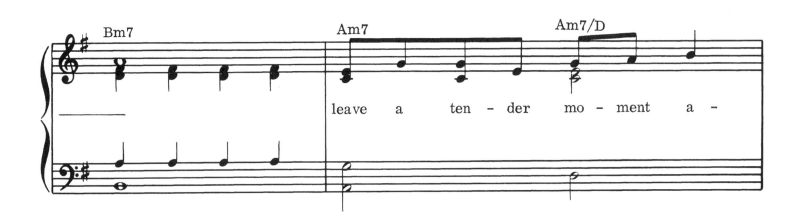

leave a ten - der mo - ment a -

lone. 2. Yes, I know I'm in love. But it's not on - ly

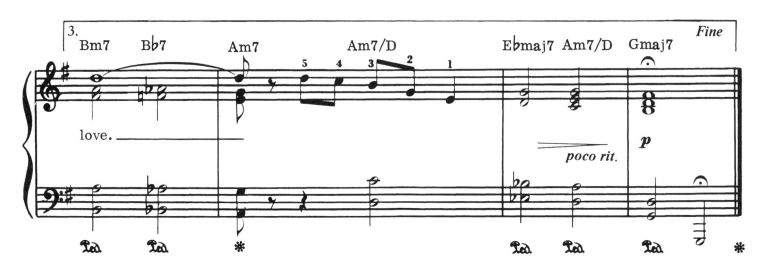

love. _____

me break-ing down____ when the ten-sion gets high;____

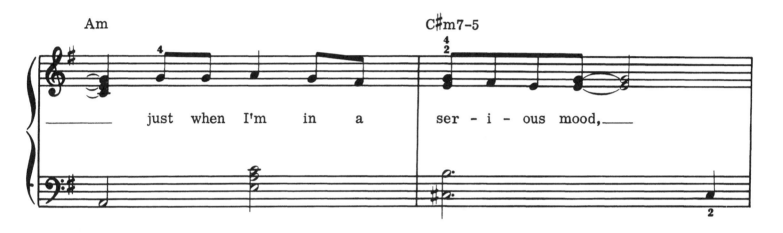

____ just when I'm in a ser - i - ous mood,____

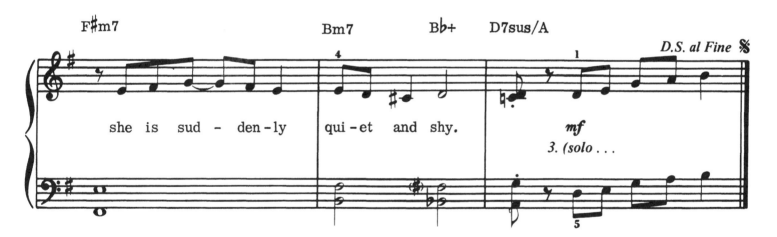

she is sud - den-ly qui - et and shy.

mf

3. (solo . . .

Verse 2:

Yes, I know I'm in love, but just when I ought to relax,
I put my foot in my mouth, 'cause I'm **just avoiding the facts.**
If the girl gets too close: if I need some room to escape;
When a moment arose, I'd tell her it's all a mistake;
But that's not how I feel; no, that's not the woman I've known.
She's undeniably real, so leave a tender moment alone.

Verse 3: (measures 1 - 7: solo)

I know the moment isn't right to hold my emotions inside;
To change the attitude tonight, I've run out of places to hide.
And if that's how I feel, then it's the best feeling I've ever known.
It's undeniably real; leave a tender moment alone.

TELL HER ABOUT IT

Words and Music by
BILLY JOEL

With a driving beat ♩ = 152

12

Verse 2:
Listen boy, I'm sure that you think you got it all under control.
You don't want somebody telling you the way to stay in someone's soul.
You're a big boy now, and you'll never let her go;
But that's just the kind of thing she ought to know. _(To Chorus:)_

Verse 3:
Listen boy, it's not automatically a certain guarantee;
To insure yourself, you've got to provide communication constantly.
When you love someone you're always insecure;
And there's only one good way to reassure. _(To Chorus:)_

Chorus 3:
Tell her about it, let her know how much you care.
When she can't be with you tell her you wish you were there.

Chorus 4:
Tell her about it, every day before you leave.
Pay her some attention, give her something to believe.

Verse 4:
Listen boy, it's good information from a man who's made mistakes.
Just a word or two that she gets from you could be the difference that it makes.
She's a trusting soul, she's put her trust in you;
But a girl like that won't tell you what you should do. _(To Chorus:)_

IT'S STILL ROCK AND ROLL TO ME

Words and Music by
BILLY JOEL

Very Quickly, with a strong 2 feel

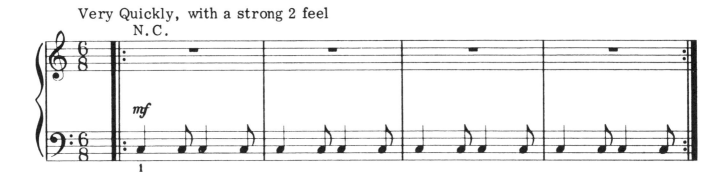

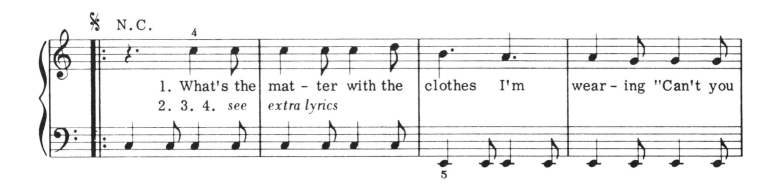

1. What's the mat-ter with the clothes I'm wear-ing "Can't you
2. 3. 4. *see extra lyrics*

tell that your tie's too wide?"

May-be I should buy some old tab col-lars?" Wel-come back to the

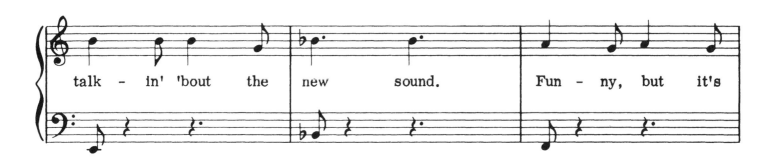

talk - in' 'bout the new sound. Fun - ny, but it's

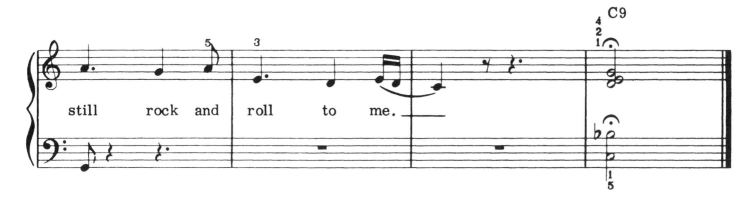

still rock and roll to me.

2. What's the matter with the car I'm driving?
"Can't you tell that it's out of style?"
Should I get a set of white wall tires?
"Are you gonna cruise the miracle mile?
Now a-days you can't be too sentimental.
Your best bet's a true baby blue Continental."
Hot funk, cool punk even if it's old junk,
It's still rock and roll to me.

3. How about a pair of pink sidewinders
And a bright orange pair of pants?
"Well, you could really be a Beau Brummel baby,
If you just give it half a chance.
Don't waste your money on a new set of speakers.
You get more mileage from a cheap pair of sneakers."
Next phase, new wave, dance craze; anyways
It's still rock and roll to me.

4. What's the matter with the crowd I'm seeing?
"Don't you know that they're out of touch?"
Should I try to be a straight 'A' student?
"If you are, then you think too much."
"Don't ya know about the new fashion, honey?
All you need are looks and a whole lot of money."
It's the next phase, new wave, dance craze; anyways
It's still rock and roll to me.

BABY GRAND

Words and Music by
BILLY JOEL

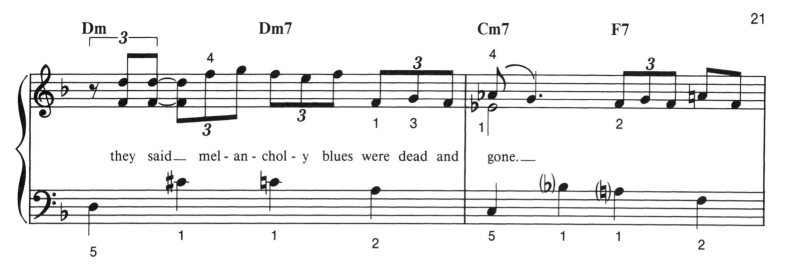

they said_ mel - an - chol - y blues were dead and gone._

But__ on - ly songs like these,_ played in mi - nor keys,

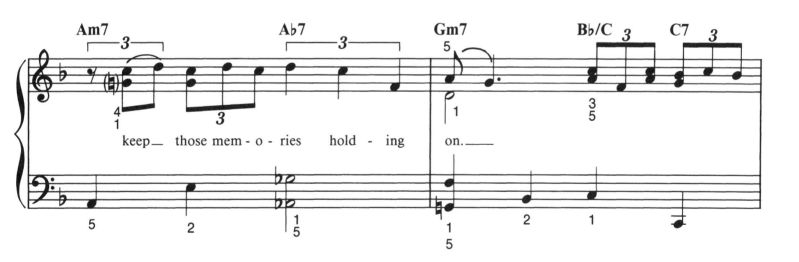

keep_ those mem - o - ries hold - ing on._

I've come far from the life I strayed in; I've got scars

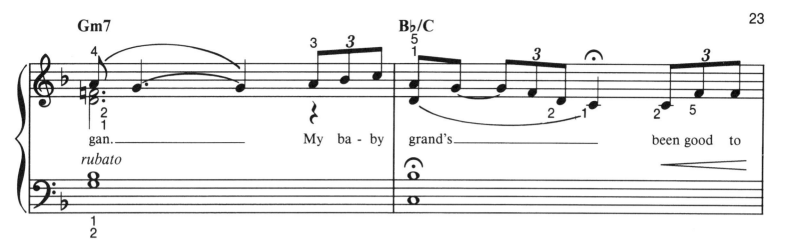

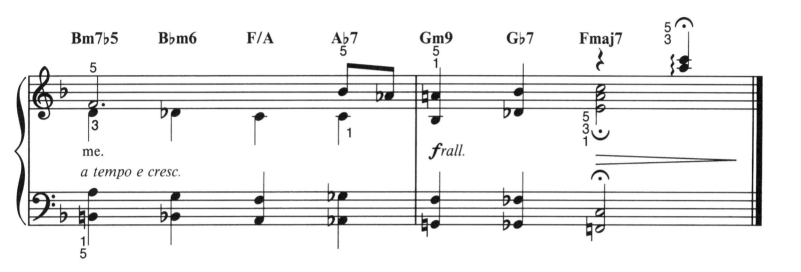

Additional Lyrics

2. In my time, I've wandered everywhere
   Around this world; she would always be there,
   Any day, any hour;
   All it takes is the power in my hands.
   This baby grand's been good to me.

3. I've had friends, but they slipped away.
   I've had fame, but it doesn't stay.
   I've made fortunes, spent them fast enough.
   As for women, they don't last with just one man;
   But Baby Grand will stand by me.

   (To Bridge:)

THE ENTERTAINER

Words and Music by
BILLY JOEL

3. I am the entertainer, been all around the world,
I've played all kinds of palaces and met all kinds of girls.
I can't remember faces, I don't remember names,
But what the hell, you know it's just as well
'Cause after a while and a thousand miles
It all becomes the same.

4. I am the entertainer, I bring to you my songs,
I'd like to spend a day or two but I can't stay that long.
I got to meet expenses, I got to stay in line,
Got to get those fees to the agencies
And I'd love to stay but there's bills to pay
So I just don't have the time.

5. I am the entertainer, I've come to do my show,
You've heard my latest record spin on the radio.
It took me years to write it, they were the best years of my life,
If you're gonna have a hit you gotta make it fit
So they cut it down to 3:05.

6. I am the entertainer, the idol of my age,
I make all kinds of money when I go on the stage.
You see me in the papers, I've been in the magazines,
But if I go cold, I won't get sold,
I get put in the back in the discount rack
Like another can of beans.

7. I am the entertainer and I know just where I stand,
Another serenader and another long-haired band.
Today I am your champion, I may have won your hearts,
But I know the game, you'll forget my name,
I won't be here in another year
If I don't stay on the charts.

THIS IS THE TIME

Words and Music by
BILLY JOEL

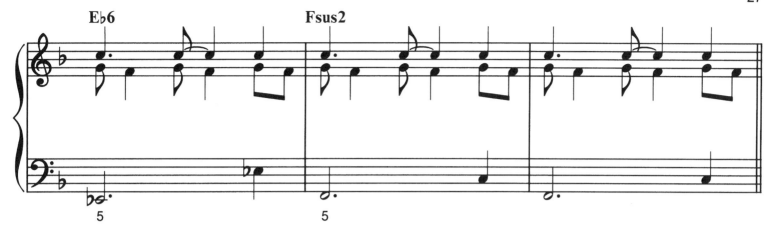

Verse

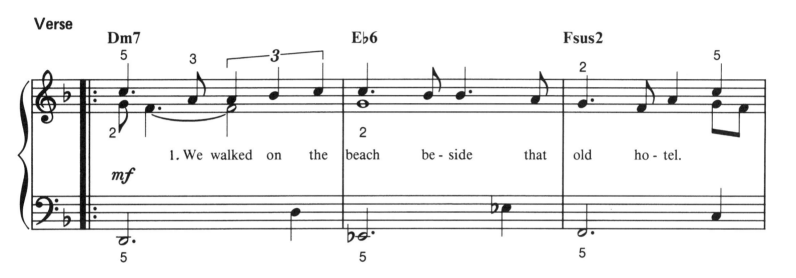

1. We walked on the beach be - side that old ho - tel.

They're tear - in' it down now,___ but it's

just as well. I have - n't shown you

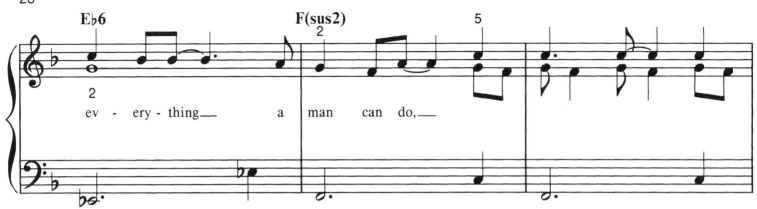

ev - ery - thing___ a man can do,___

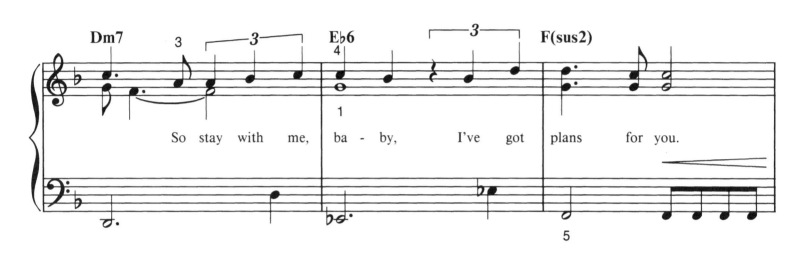

So stay with me, ba - by, I've got plans for you.

Chorus:

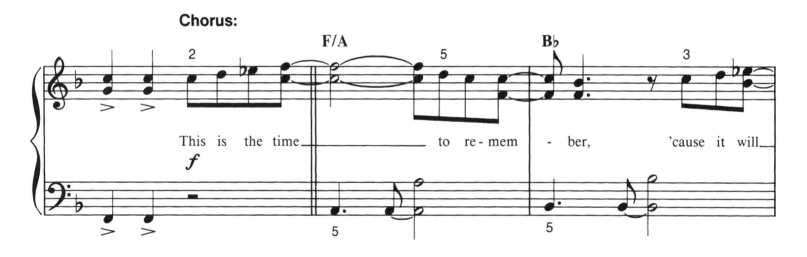

This is the time___ to re - mem - ber, 'cause it will___

___ not last___ for - ev - er. These are the days___ to hold on___

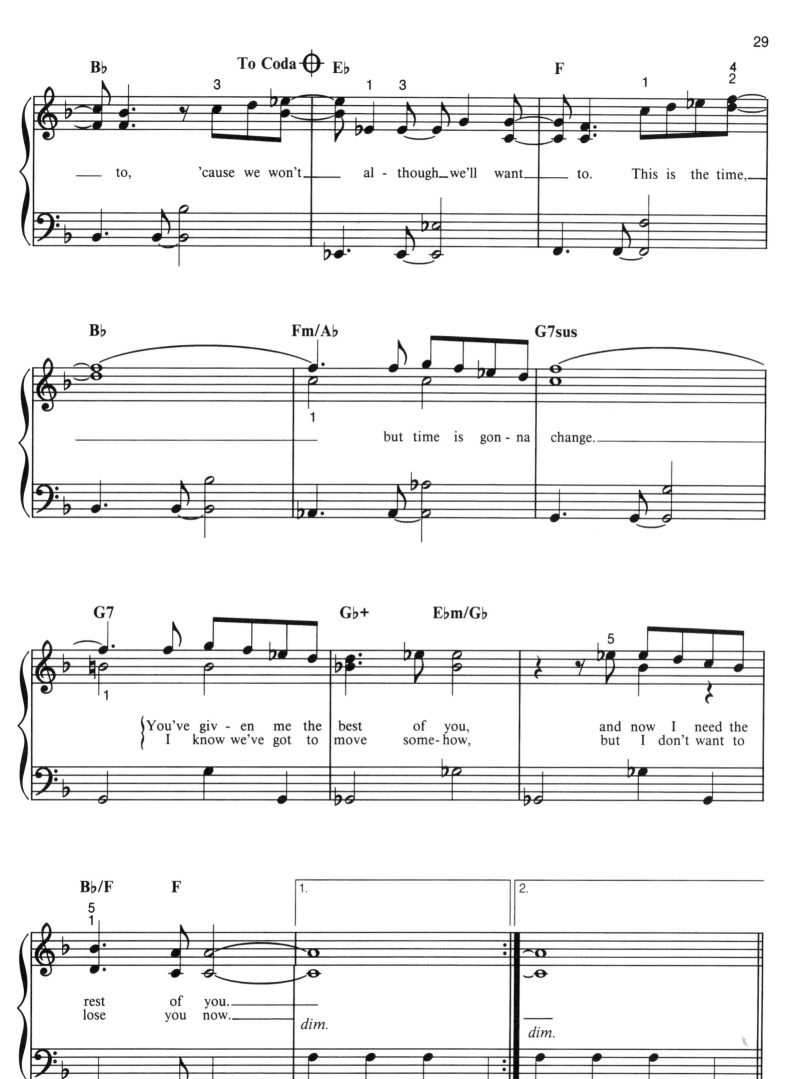

30

Bridge:

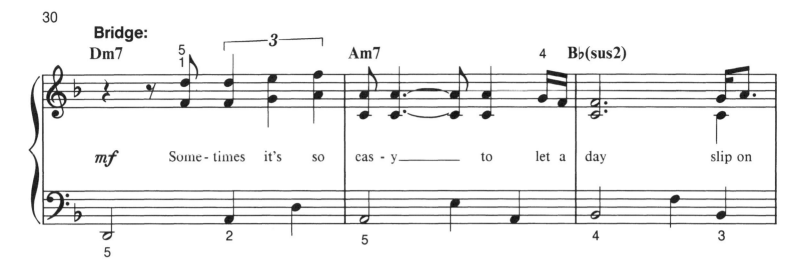

Some-times it's so eas-y_____ to let a day slip on

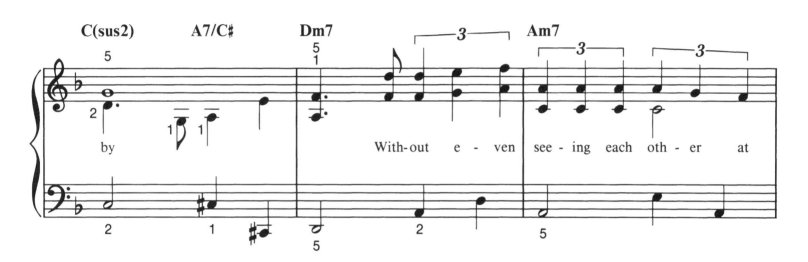

by Without e - ven see-ing each oth - er at

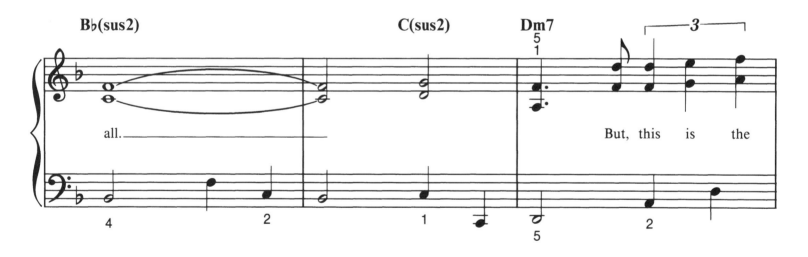

all._____ But, this is the

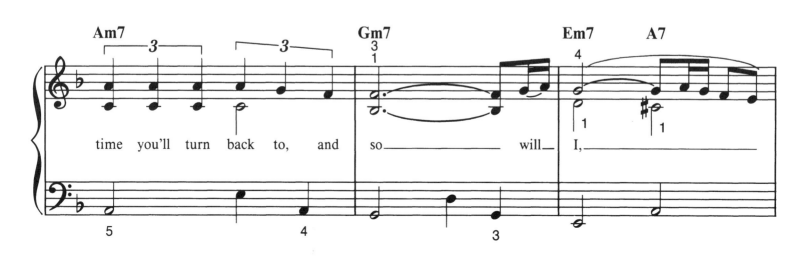

time you'll turn back to, and so_____ will I,_____

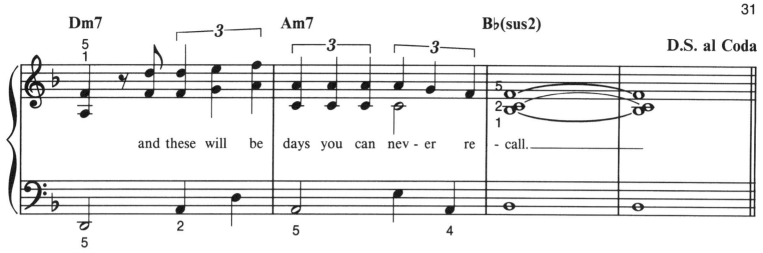

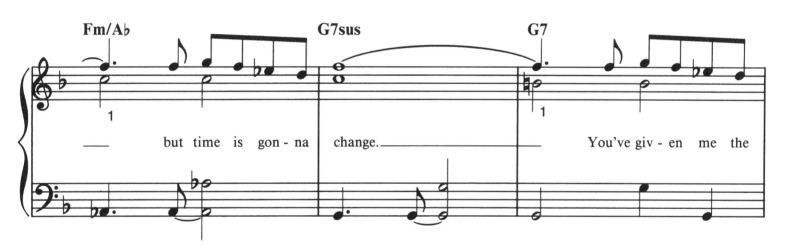

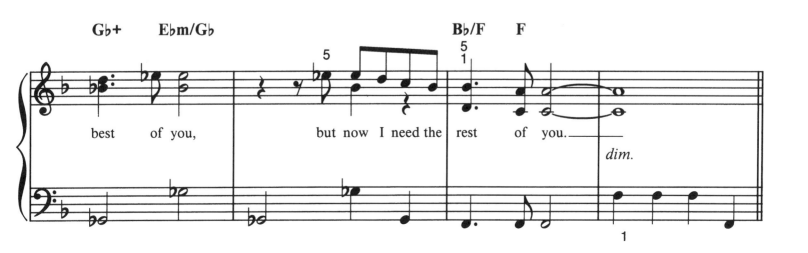

Additional Lyrics

2. Did you know that before you came into my life,
   It was some kind of miracle that I survived.
   Someday, we will both look back and have to laugh.
   We lived through a lifetime and the aftermath.

   (To Chorus:)

3. And so we embrace again behind the dunes.
   This beach is so cold on winter afternoons.
   But holding you close is like holding the summer sun.
   I'm warm from the memory of days to come.

   (To Chorus:)

SHE'S ALWAYS A WOMAN

Words and Music by
BILLY JOEL

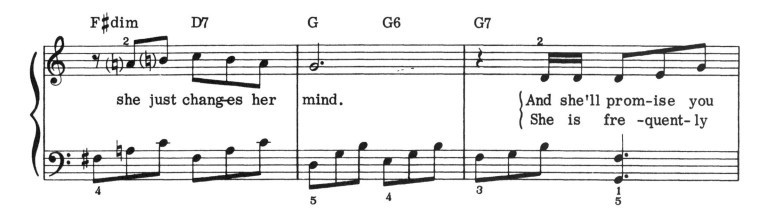

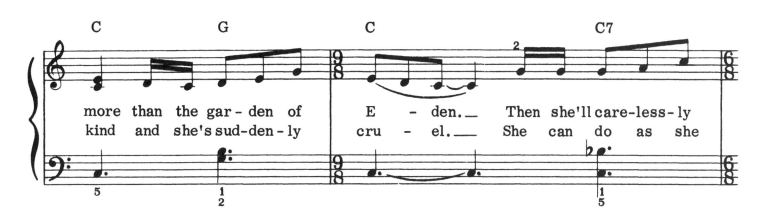

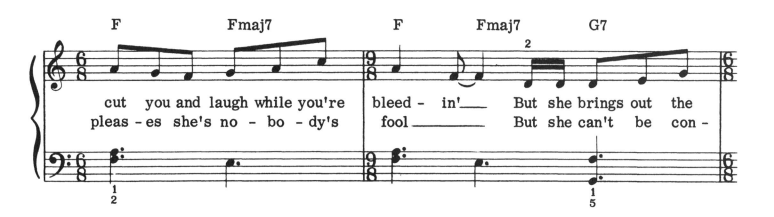

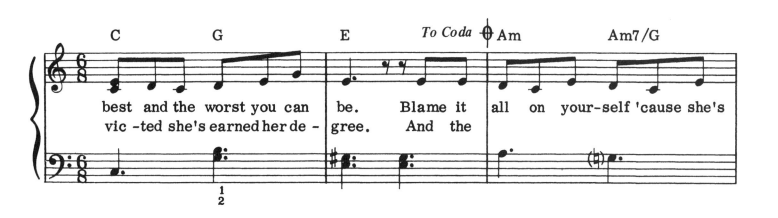

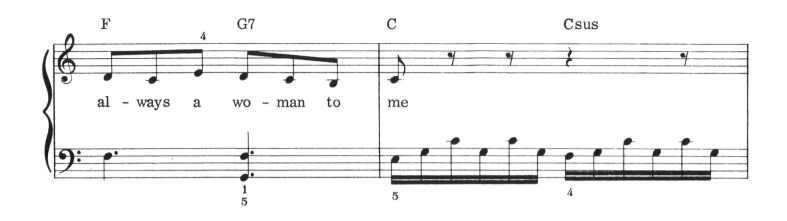

al - ways   a   wo - man   to   me

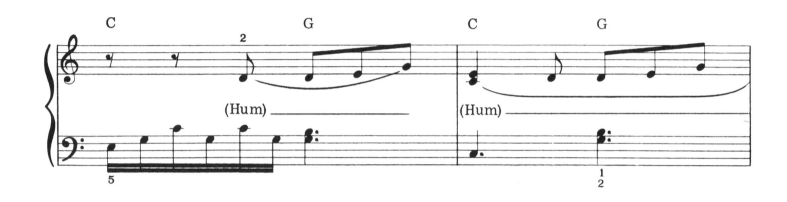

(Hum) _____   (Hum) _____

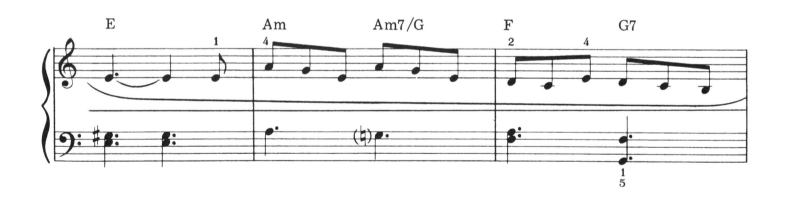

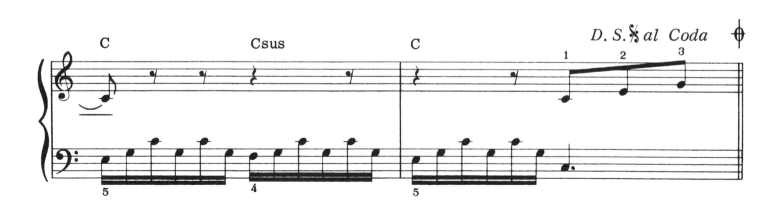

D. S. 𝄋 *al Coda*

37

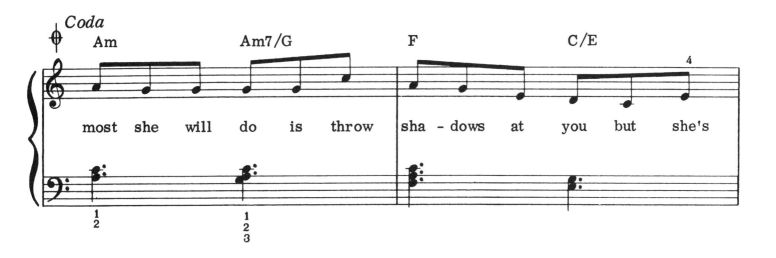

most she will do is throw sha - dows at you but she's

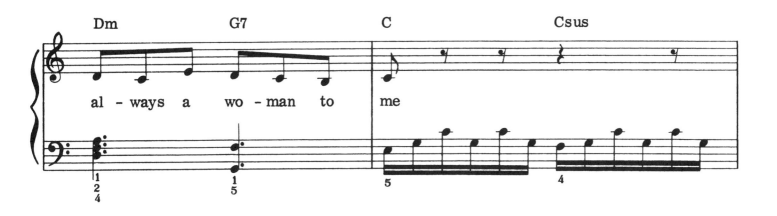

al - ways a wo - man to me

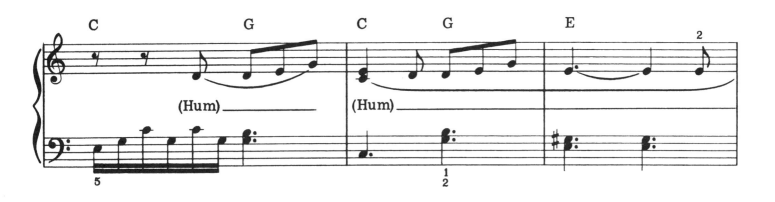

(Hum) _____ (Hum) _____

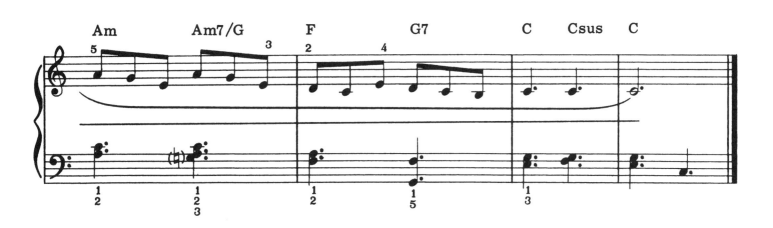

HONESTY

Words and Music by
BILLY JOEL

Slowly, in 2

1. If you search for ten-der-ness,— it is-n't hard to
2,3. See extra lyrics

find.— You can have the love— you need to live.

And if you look for truth-

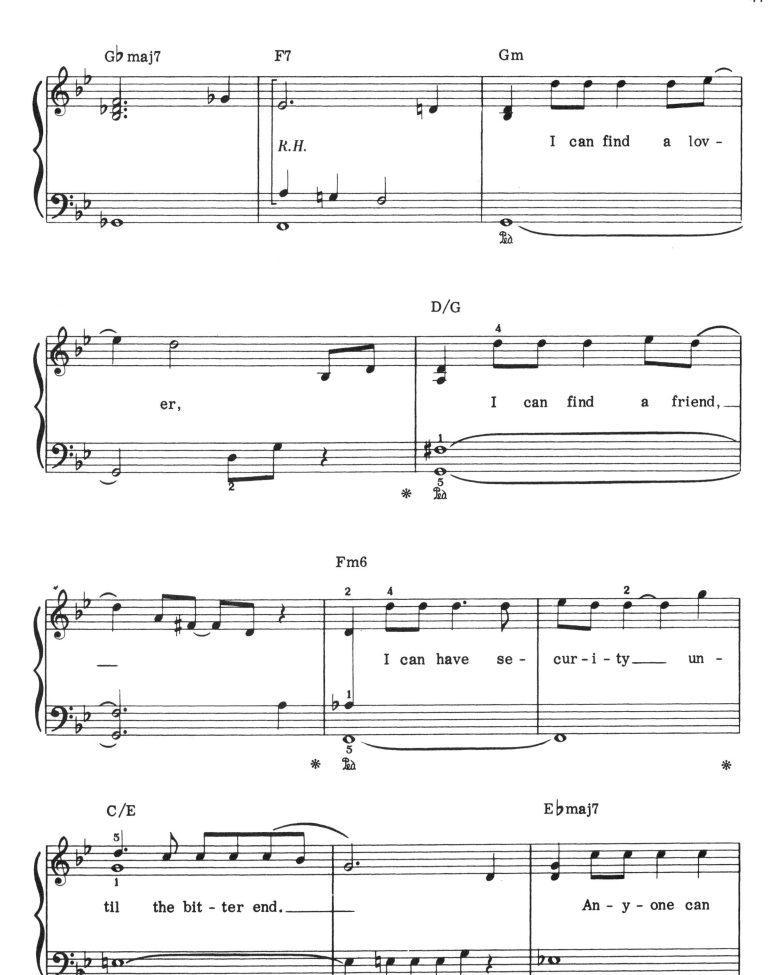

42

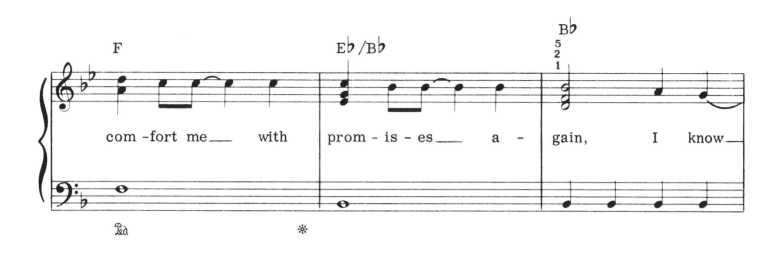

com -fort me ___ with prom - is - es ___ a - gain, I know ___

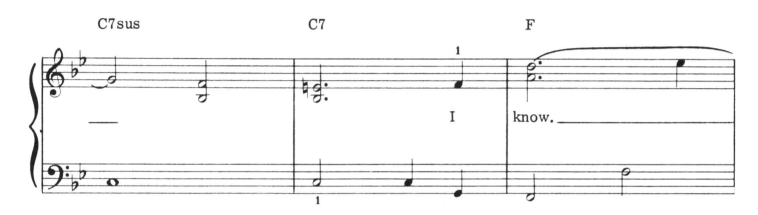

___ I know. ___

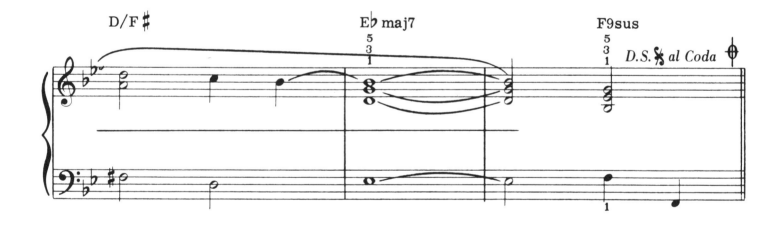

D.S. 𝄋 al Coda ⊕

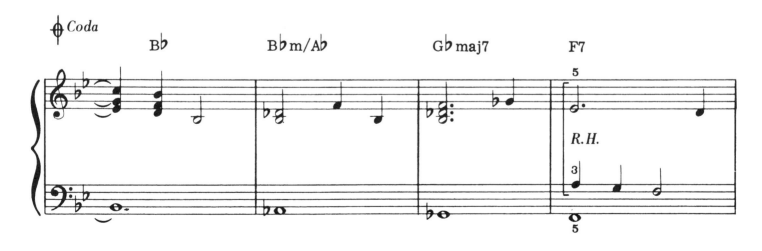

⊕ Coda

R.H.

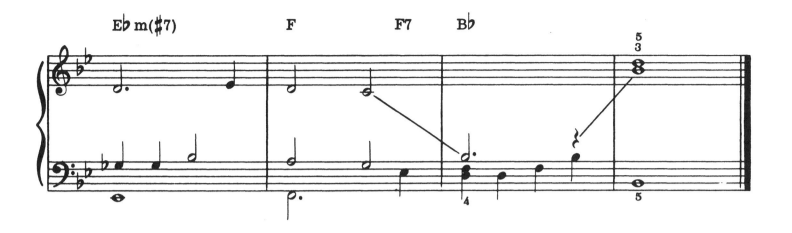

2. I can always find someone
   To say they sympathize
   If I wear my heart out on my sleeve
   But I don't want some pretty face
   To tell me pretty lies
   All I want is someone to believe

   Chorus

3. When I'm deep inside of me
   Don't be too concerned
   I won't ask for nothin' while I'm gone
   When I want sincerity
   Tell me where else can I turn
   Cause you're the one that I depend upon

   Chorus

PIANO MAN

Word and Music by
BILLY JOEL

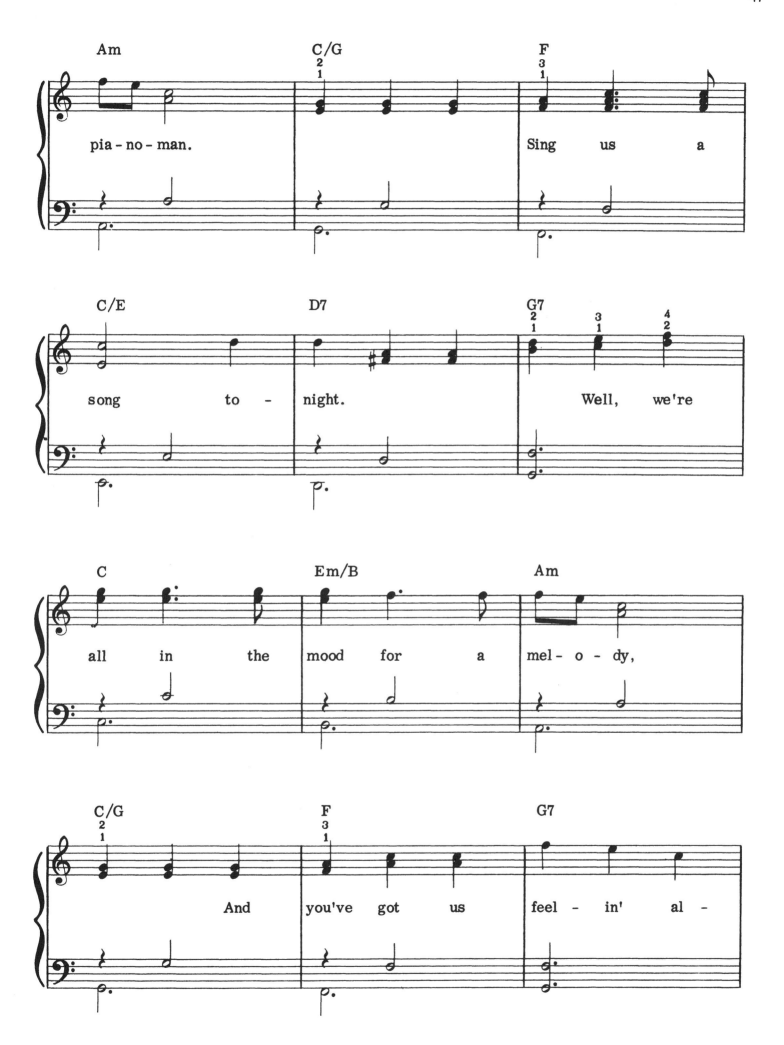

48

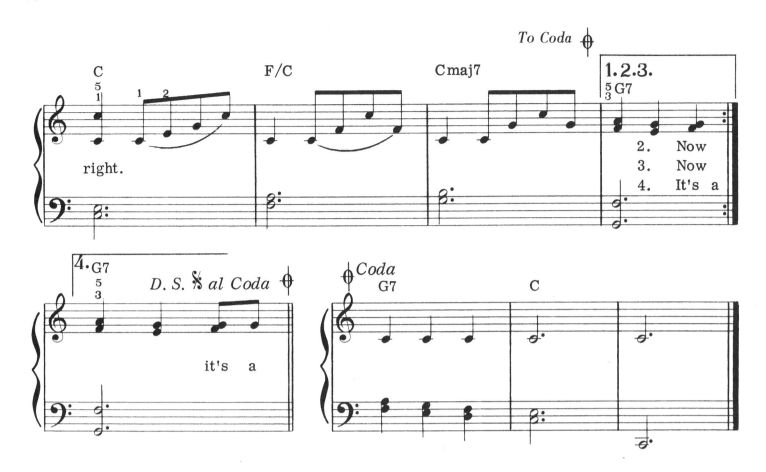

2. Now John at the bar is a friend of mine,
   He gets me my drinks for free,
   And he's quick with a joke or to light up your smoke
   But there's someplace that he'd rather be.
   He says, "Bill, I believe this is killing me,"
   As a smile ran away from his face
   "Well, I'm sure that I could be a movie star
   If I could get out of this place."

3. Now Paul is a real estate novelist
   Who never had time for a wife
   And he's talkin' with Davy who's still in the Navy
   And probably will be for life.
   And the waitress is practicing politics,
   As the businessmen slowly get stoned
   Yes, they're sharing a drink they call loneliness
   But it's better than drinkin' alone.

4. It's a pretty good crowd for a Saturday,
   And the manager gives me a smile
   'Cause he knows that it's me they've been comin' to see
   To forget about life for a while.
   And the piano sounds like a carnival
   And the microphone smells like a beer
   And they sit at the bar and put bread in my jar
   And say "Man, what are you doin' here?"

SAY GOODBYE TO HOLLYWOOD

Words and Music by
BILLY JOEL

Fast Rock and Roll

Bob - by's driv-in' through the cit - y to-night ___ through the lights ___
John-ny's tak-in' care of things for a while ___ and his style ___

___ in a hot ___ new rent - a -car. ___ He joins the lov-ers in his
___ is so right ___ for trou -ba-dours. ___ they got him sit-ting with his

heav-y ma-chine, ___ it's a scene ___ down on Sun - set
back to the door ___ and he won't ___ be my fast - gun

50

So many faces, in and out of my life
Some will last, some will be just now and then
Life is a series of hellos and goodbyes
I'm afraid it's time for goodbye again.

MOVIN' OUT (ANTHONY'S SONG)

Words and Music by
BILLY JOEL

Moderate

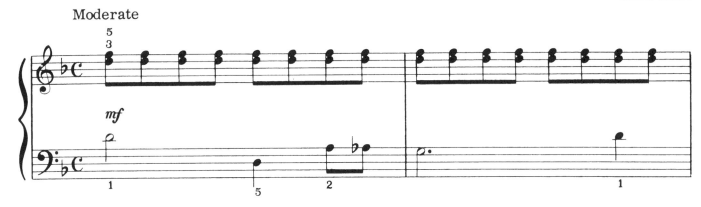

An- tho - ny works___ in the gro - cer - y store___
Ser-geant O'-Leary___ is walk-in'___ the beat___ At

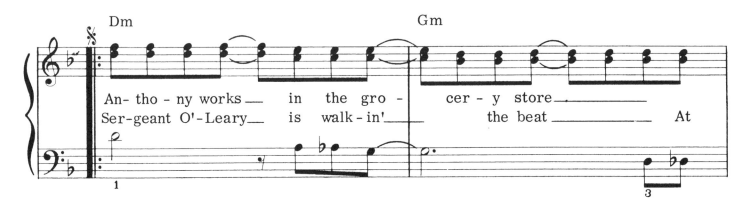

Sav - in' his pen - nies for some - day___
night he be-comes___ a bar ten - der___ He works at

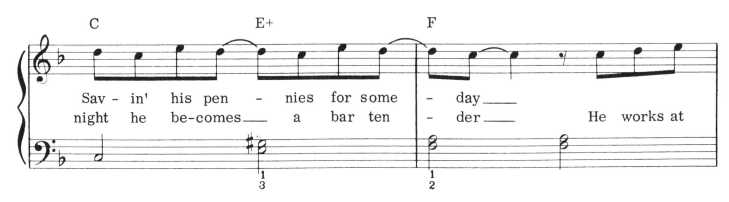

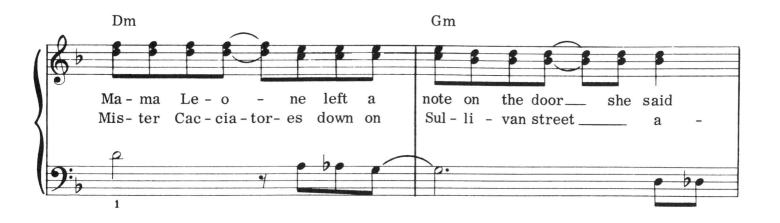

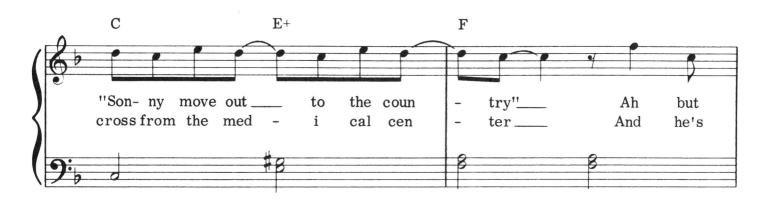

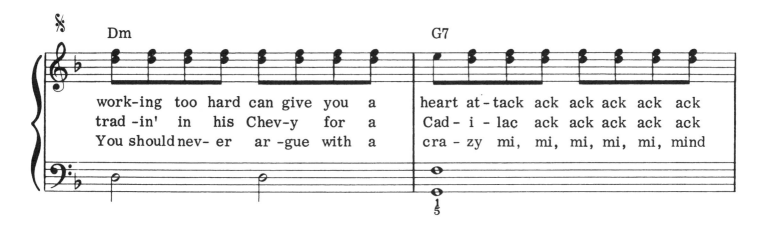

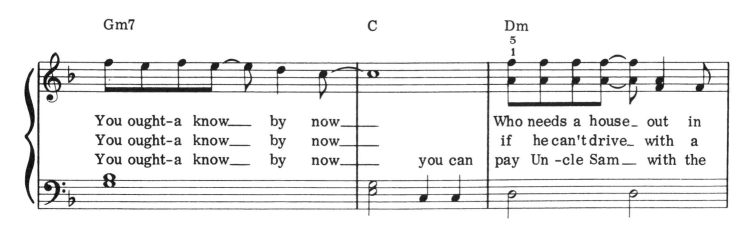

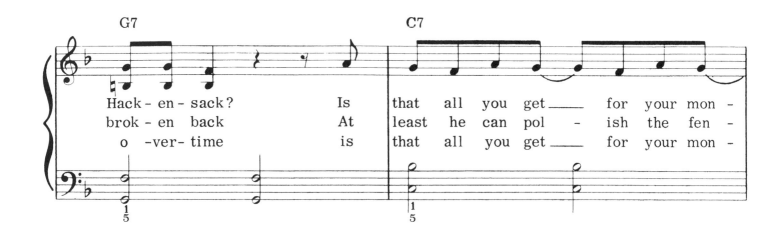

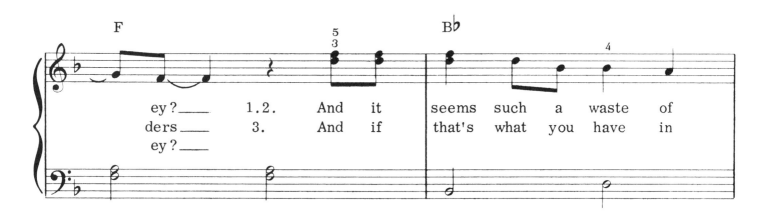

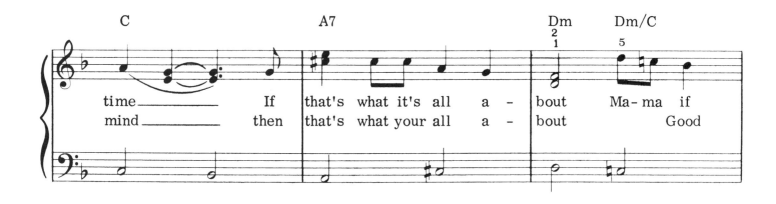

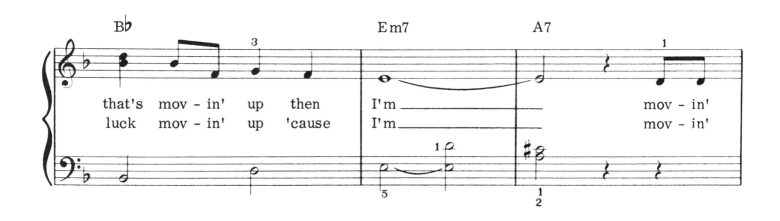

ALLENTOWN

Words and Music by
BILLY JOEL

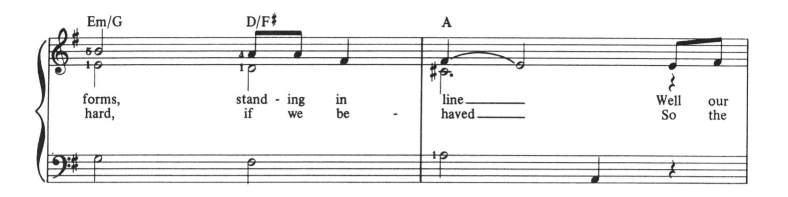

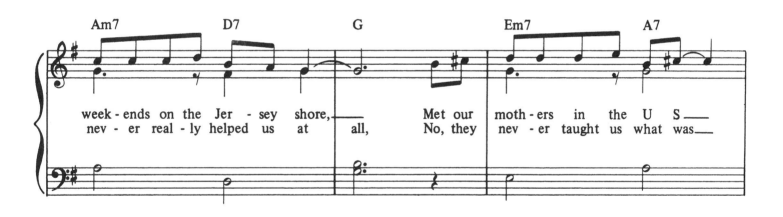

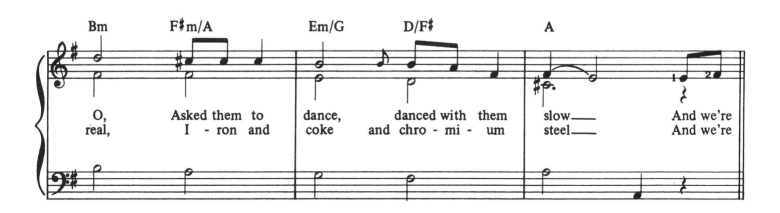

58

NEW YORK STATE OF MIND

Words and Music by
BILLY JOEL

Slowly, with a blues feel

1. Some folks____ like to get a - way take a
2. I've seen____ all the mov-ie stars in their
3.5. Comes down____ to re - al - i - ty And it's
4. *Instrumental*

hol - i - day   from the   neigh-bor-hood,   Hop a flight to Mi -
fan-cy cars   and their   lim - ou -sines,   Been high in the
fine with me,   'cause I've   let it slide   Don't care if it's

am - i Beach   or to   Hol - ly - wood
Rock-ies   un - der the   ev - er - greens.
Chi - na - town   or on   Riv - er - side

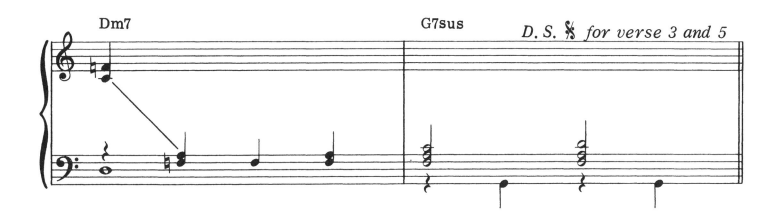

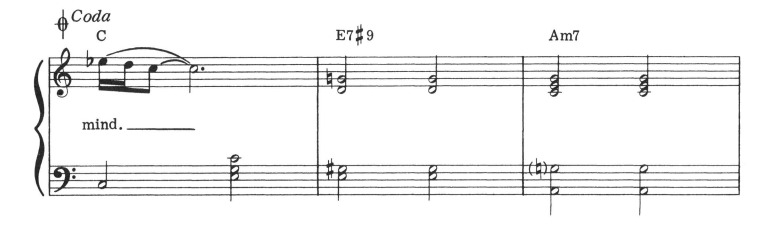

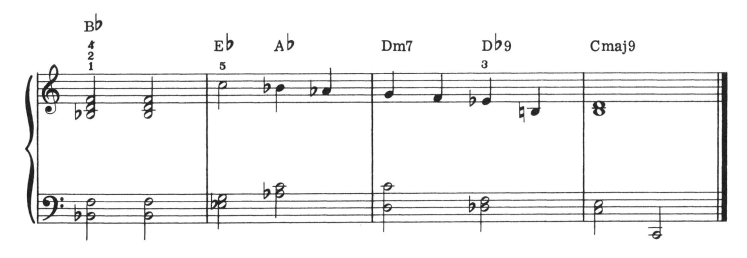

MY LIFE

Words and Music by
BILLY JOEL

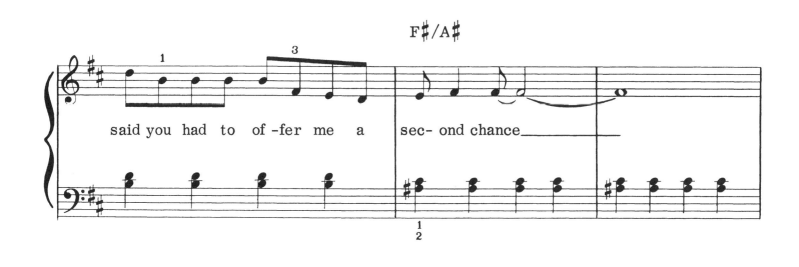

said you had to of-fer me a sec-ond chance

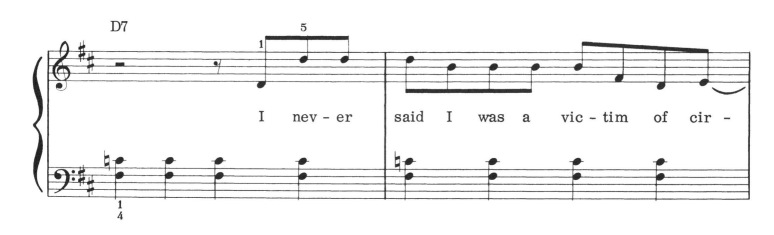

I nev-er said I was a vic-tim of cir-

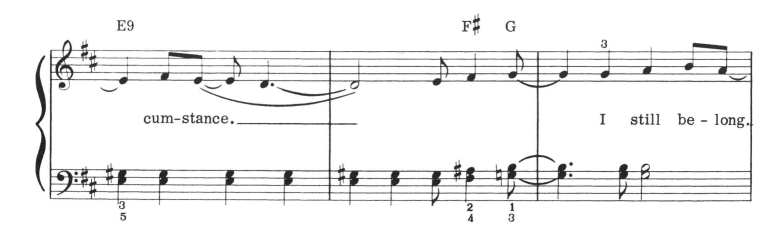

cum-stance. I still be-long.

Don't get me wrong.

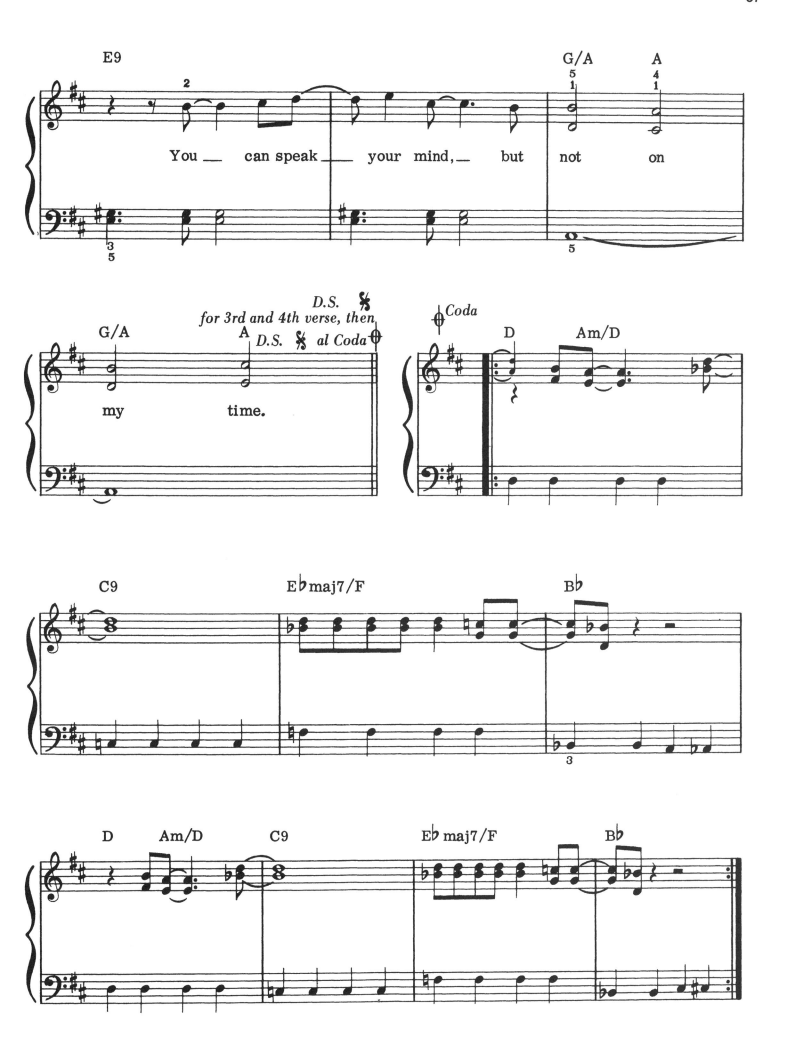

THE STRANGER

Words and Music by
BILLY JOEL

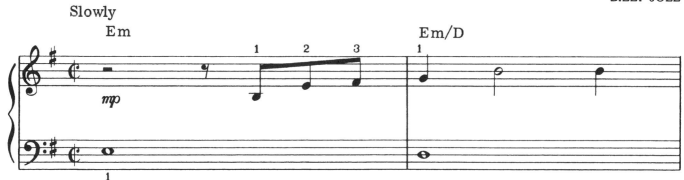

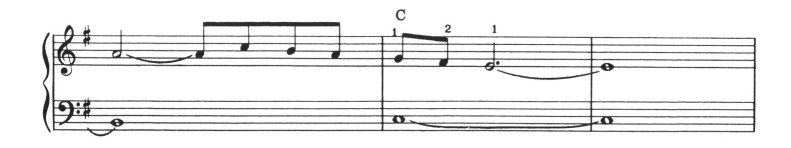

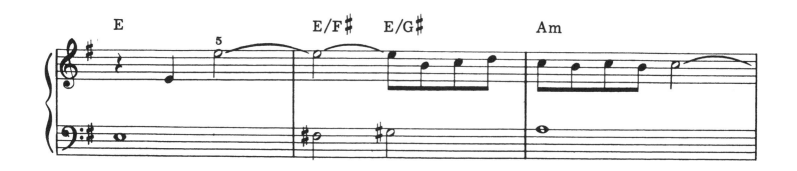

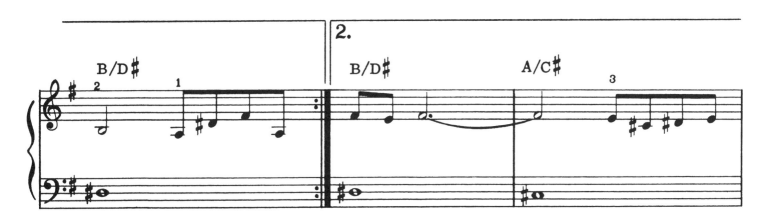

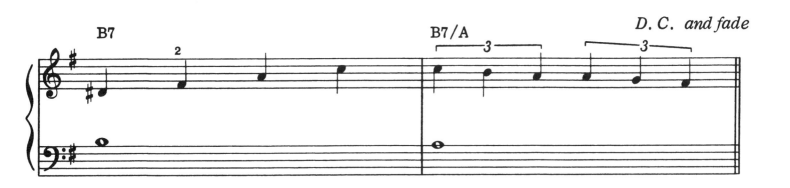

THE STRANGER

Words and Music by
BILLY JOEL

2. Once I used to believe
I was such a great romancer,
Then I came home to a woman that I could not recognize
When I pressed her for a reason she refused to even answer,
It was **then** I felt the stranger kick me right between the eyes.

3. You may never understand
How the stranger is inspired
But he isn't always evil and he isn't always wrong,
Though you drown in good intentions you will never quench the fire
You'll give in to your desires when the stranger comes along.

DON'T ASK ME WHY

Words and Music by
BILLY JOEL

74

2. All your life you had to stand in line
   Still you're standing on your feet
   All your choices made you change your mind
   Now your calendar's complete
   Don't wait for answers
   Just take your chances
   Don't ask me why

3. All the servants in your new hotel
   Throw their roses at your feet
   Fool them all but baby I can tell
   You're no stranger to the street
   Don't ask for favors
   Don't talk to strangers
   Don't ask me why

4. Yesterday you were an only child
   Now your ghosts have gone away
   You can kill them in the classic style
   Now you, "parlez vous francais"
   Don't look for answers
   You took your chances
   Don't ask me why
   Don't ask me why

YOU MAY BE RIGHT

Words and Music by
BILLY JOEL

Moderate Rock

C7sus

1. Fri - day night __ I crashed __
2. - 4. *See extra lyrics*
5. *Instrumental*

__ your par - ty, Sat - ur - day __ I said

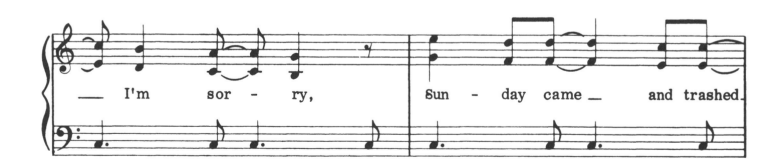

__ I'm sor - ry, Sun - day came __ and trashed

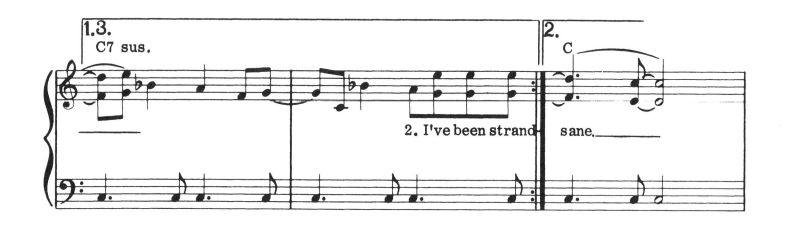

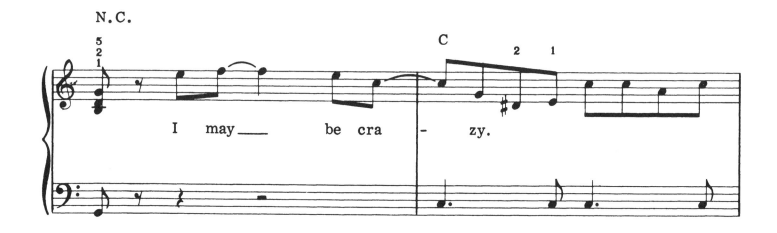

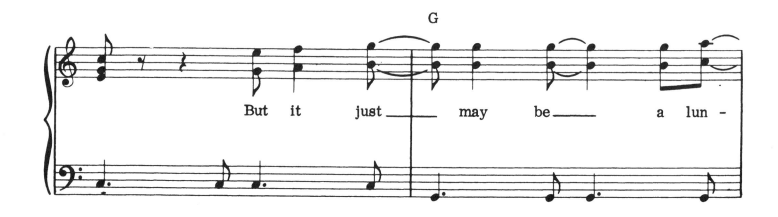

81

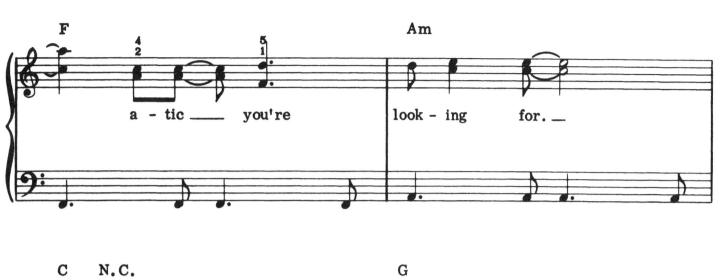

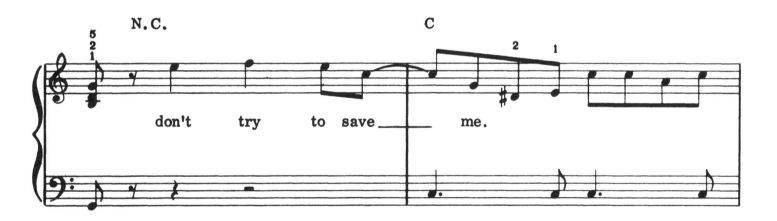

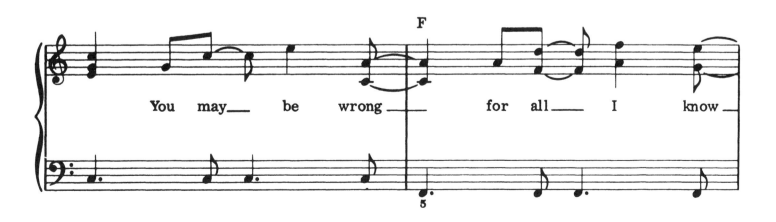

82

You may be wrong but you may be right.___

I've been stranded in the combat zone
I walked through Bedford Stuy alone
Even rode my motorcycle in the rain
And you told me not to drive
But I made it home alive
So you said that only proves that I'm insane

CHORUS:

Remember how I found you there
Alone in your electric chair
I told you dirty jokes until you smiled
You were lonely for a man
I said take me as I am
'Cause you might enjoy some madness for awhile

Now think of all the years you tried to
Find someone to satisfy you
I might be as crazy as you say
If I'm crazy then it's true
That it's all because of you
And you wouldn't want me any other way

CHORUS:

UPTOWN GIRL

Moderately, with a steady beat

Words and Music by
BILLY JOEL

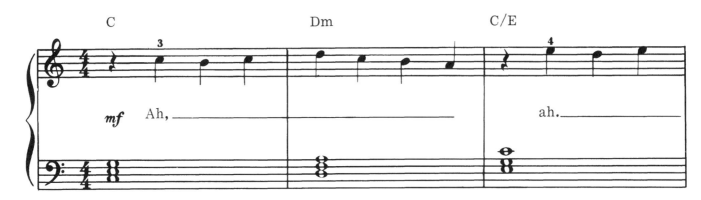

Ah, _____ ah. _____

_____ Up town girl,
2.3.(See additional lyrics)
she's been liv-ing in her

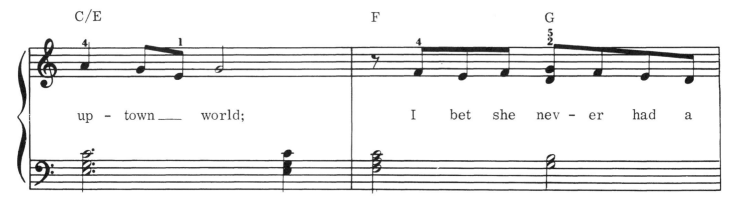

up - town ___ world; I bet she nev - er had a

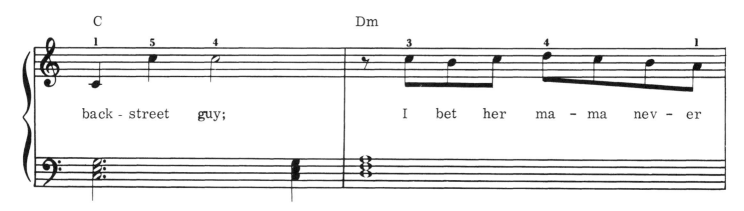

back - street guy; I bet her ma - ma nev - er

Verse 2:
I'm gonna try for an uptown girl;
She's been living in her white bread world;
As long as anyone with hot blood can;
And now she's looking for a downtown man;
That's what I am.
(To Bridge:)

Verse 3:
Uptown girl; you know I can't afford to buy her pearls;
But maybe someday when my ship comes in;
She'll understand what kind of guy I've been;
And then I'll win.

Bridge 2:
And when she's walking, she's looking so fine;
And when she's talking, she'll say that she's mine;
She'll say I'm not so tough just because I'm in love with an

Final Verse:
Uptown girl. She's been living in her white bread world;
As long as anyone with hot blood can;
And now she's looking for a downtown man;
That's what I am.
Oh . . .

THE LONGEST TIME

Words and Music by
BILLY JOEL

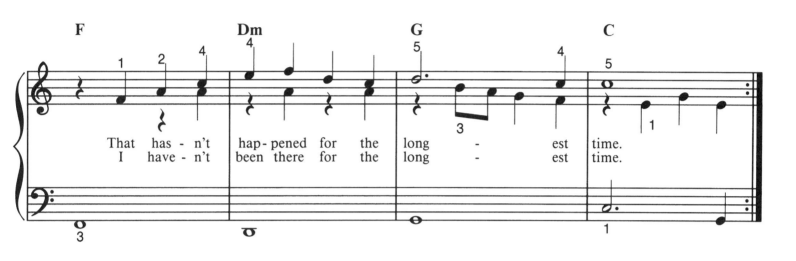

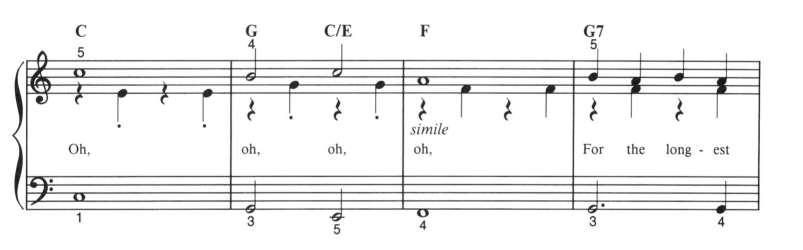

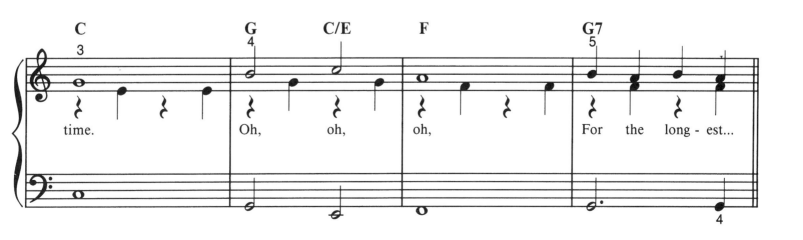

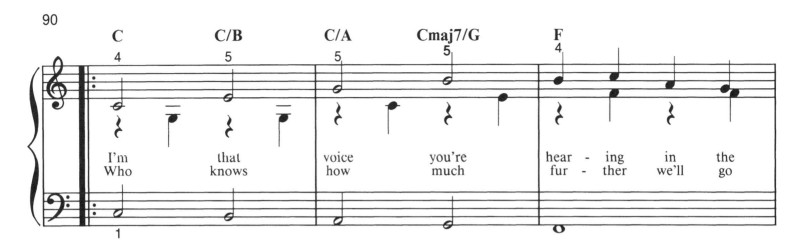

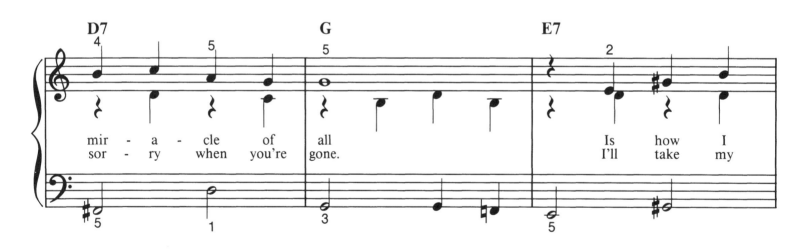

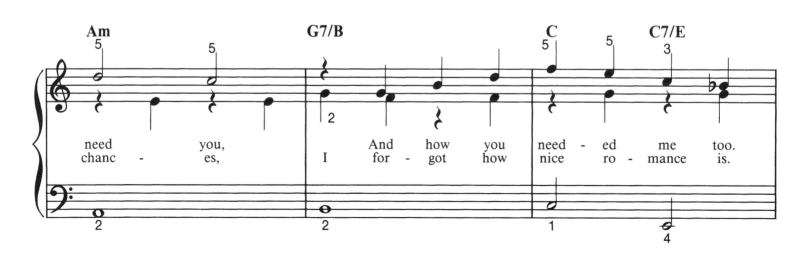

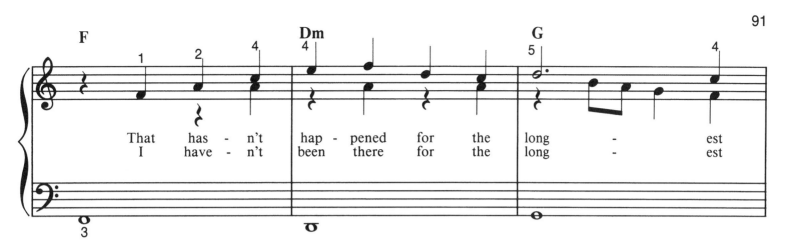

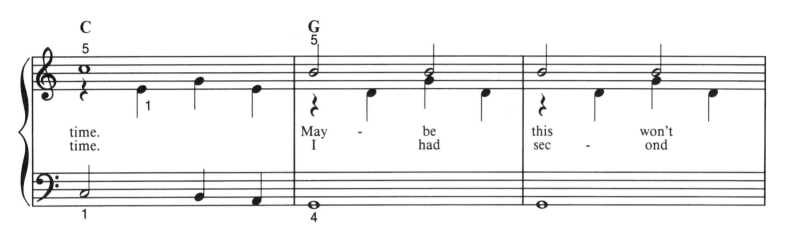

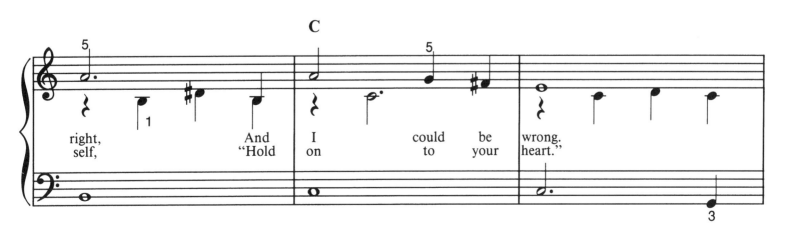

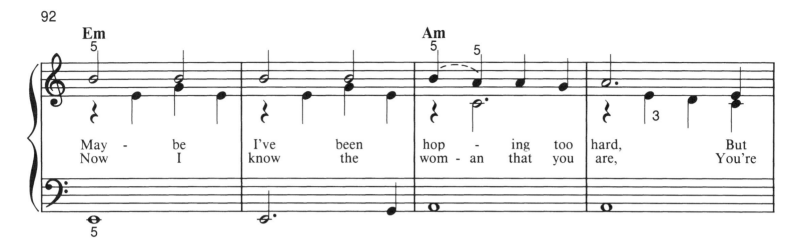

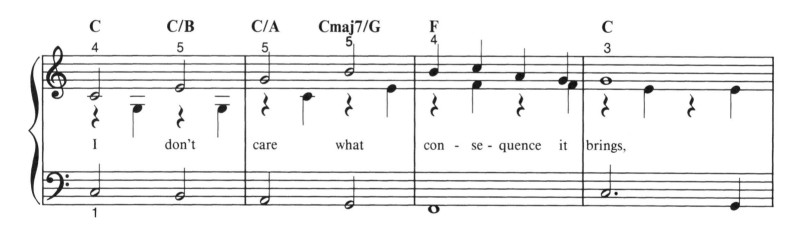

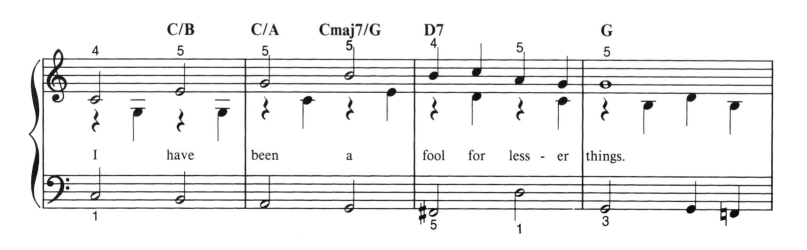

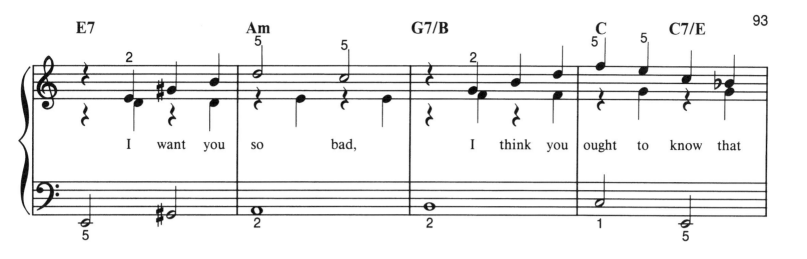

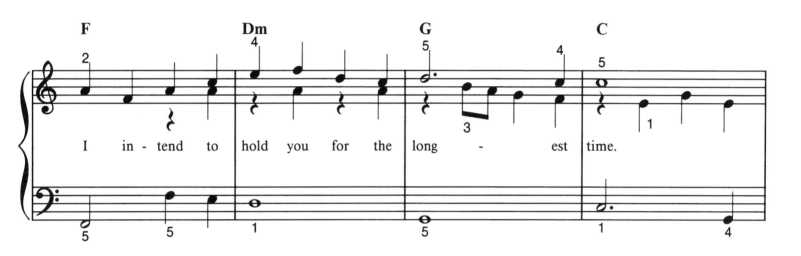

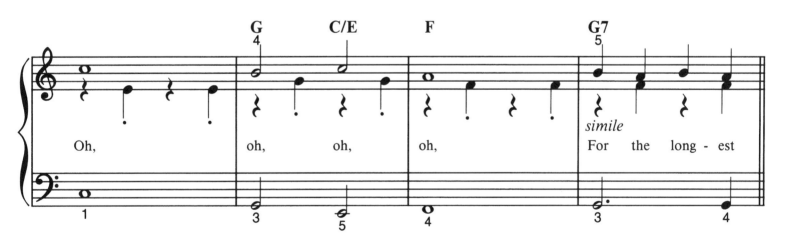

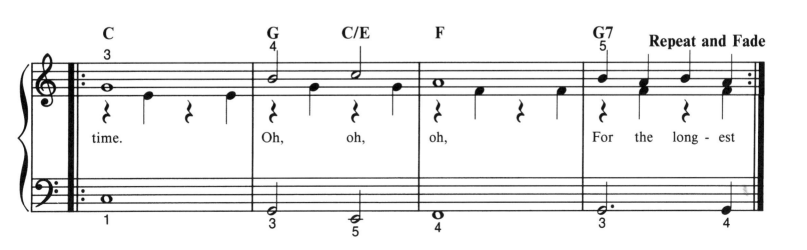

SHE'S GOT A WAY

Words and Music by
BILLY JOEL

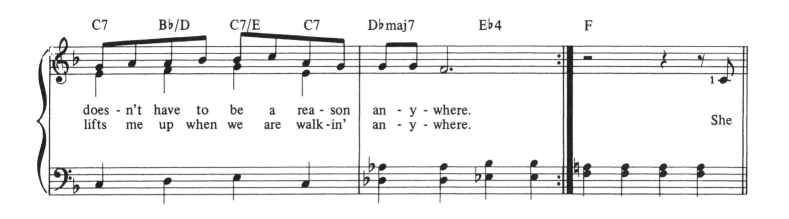

does-n't have to be a rea-son an-y-where.
lifts me up when we are walk-in' an-y-where.

She

comes to me when I'm feel-in' down,__ In-spires me with-out a sound. She

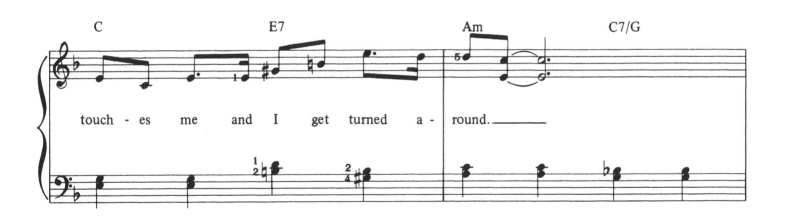

touch-es me and I get turned a-round._____

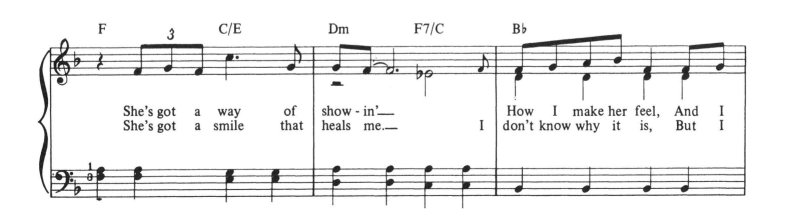

She's got a way of show-in'__
She's got a smile that heals me.__

How I make her feel, And I
I don't know why it is, But I

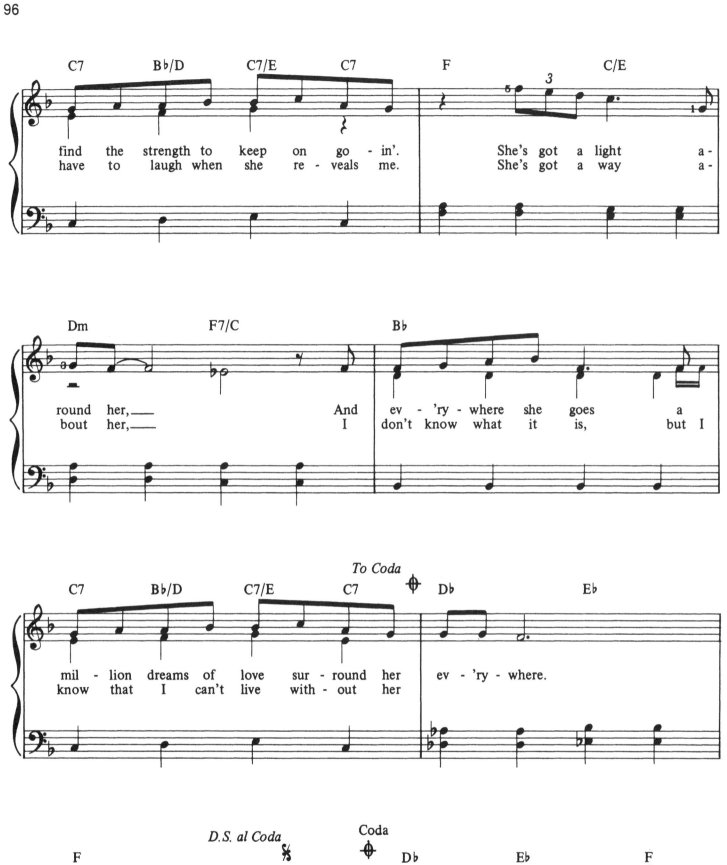